8x 1/15 CT 8/12

STONEWALL
JACKSON

Chris Hughes

BLACKBIRCH PRESS, INC.

WOODBRIDGE, CONNECTICUT

Published by Blackbirch Press, Inc.
260 Amity Road
Woodbridge, CT 06525
Web site: http://www.blackbirch.com
e-mail: staff@blackbirch.com
© 2001 Blackbirch Press, Inc.

Printed in China

10 9 8 7 6 5 4 3 2 1

Photo credits:
Cover, back cover, pages, 4, 9, 18, 37, 54, 66, 67, 73, 86, 91, 93: (c)North
Wind Picture Archives; pages 6, 29: Blackbirch Press; pages 10, 15, 26, 34,
59, 60, 64, 70, 80, 89: The Library of Congress; pages 17, 38, 45, 51, 84,
97: National Archives; pages 22, 30, 32, 94, 100: courtesy Virginia Military
Institute Archives; page 42: National Portrait Gallery.

Library of Congress Cataloging-in-Publication Data
Hughes, Christopher (Christopher A.), 1968–
Thomas Stonewall Jackson / by Chris Hughes.
        p. cm. — (The Civil War)
Includes index.
            ISBN 1-56711-559-4
1. Jackson, Stonewall, 1824–1863—Juvenile literature. 2. Generals—
Confederate States of America—Biography—Juvenile literature.
3.Confederate States of America. Army—Biography—Juvenile literature.
4. United States—History—Civil War, 1861–1865—Campaigns—Juvenile
literature. [1. Jackson, Stonewall, 1824–1863. 2. Generals. 3. United States—
History—Civil War, 1861–1865.] I. Title. II. Civil War (Blackbirch Press)
E467.1.J15 H84 2001
973.7'3'092—dc21   2001001573

CONTENTS

PREFACE: THE CIVIL WAR

Nearly 150 years after the final shots were fired, the Civil War remains one of the key events in U. S. history. The enormous loss of life alone makes it tragically unique: More Americans died in Civil War battles than in all other American wars combined. More Americans fell at the Battle of Gettysburg than during any battle in American military history. And, in one day at the Battle of Antietam, more Americans were killed and wounded than in any other day in American history.

As tragic as the loss of life was, however, it is the principles over which the war was fought that make it uniquely American. Those beliefs—equality and freedom—are the foundation of American democracy, our basic rights. It was the bitter disagreement about the exact nature of those rights that drove our nation to its bloodiest war.

The disagreements grew in part from the differing economies of the North and South. The warm climate and wide-open areas of the Southern states were ideal for an economy based on agriculture. In the first half of the 19th century, the main cash crop was cotton,

Slaves did the backbreaking work on Southern plantations.

grown on large farms called plantations. Slaves, who were brought to the United States from Africa, were forced to do the backbreaking work of planting and harvesting cotton. They also provided the other labor necessary to keep plantations running. Slaves were bought and sold like property, and had been critical to the Southern economy since the first Africans came to America in 1619.

The suffering of African Americans under slavery is one of the great tragedies in American history. And the debate over whether the United States government had the right to forbid slavery—in both Southern states and in new territories—was a dispute that overshadowed the first 80 years of our history.

For many Northerners, the question of slavery was one of morality and not economics. Because the Northern economy was based on manufacturing rather than agriculture, there was little need for slave labor. The primary economic need of Northern states was a protective tax known as a tariff that would make imported goods more expensive than goods made in the North. Tariffs forced Southerners to buy Northern goods and made them economically dependent on the North, a fact that led to deep resentment among Southerners.

Economic control did not matter to the anti-slavery Northerners known as abolitionists. Their conflict with the South was over slavery. The idea that the federal government could outlaw slavery was perfectly reasonable. After all, abolitionists contended, our nation was founded on the idea that all people are created equal. How could slavery exist in such a country?

For the Southern states that joined the Confederacy, the freedom from unfair taxation and the right to make their

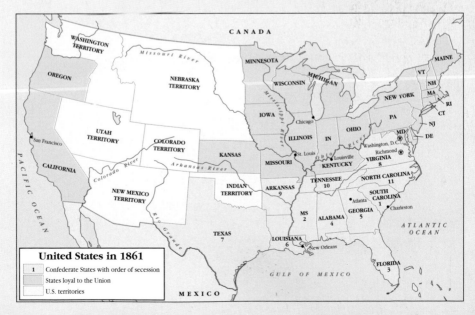

own decisions about slavery was as important a principle as equality. For most Southerners, the right of states to decide what is best for its citizens was the most important principle guaranteed in the Constitution.

The conflict over these principles generated sparks throughout the decades leading up to the Civil War. The importance of keeping an equal number of slave and free states in the Union became critical to Southern lawmakers in Congress in those years. In 1820, when Maine and Missouri sought admission to the Union, the question was settled by the Missouri Compromise: Maine was admitted as a free state, Missouri as a slave state, thus maintaining a balance in Congress. The compromise stated that all future territories north of the southern boundary of Missouri would enter the Union as free states, those south of it would be slave states.

In 1854, however, the Kansas-Nebraska Act set the stage for the Civil War. That act repealed the Missouri Compromise and by declaring that the question of slavery should be decided by residents of the territory, set off a rush of pro- and anti-slavery settlers to the new land. Violence between the two sides began almost immediately and soon "Bleeding Kansas" became a tragic chapter in our nation's story.

With Lincoln's election on an anti-slavery platform in 1860, the disagreement over the power of the federal government reached its breaking point. In early 1861, South Carolina became the first state to secede from the Union, followed by Mississippi, Florida, Alabama, Georgia, Louisiana, Virginia, Texas, North Carolina, Tennessee, and Arkansas. Those eleven states became the Confederate States of America. Confederate troops fired the first shots of the Civil War at Fort Sumter, South Carolina, on April 12, 1861. Those shots began a four-year war in which thousands of Americans—Northerners and Southerners—would give, in President Lincoln's words, "the last full measure of devotion."

OPPOSITE: The Confederate attack on Fort Sumter began the Civil War.

Introduction:
Lee's "Strong Right Arm"
★ ★ ★ ★ ★

The Confederate guards of the 18th North Carolina regiment were jumpy that night. Sounds of gunfire off in the distance had them on edge. Earlier that day—May 2, 1863—surprise attacks by Stonewall Jackson's outnumbered men had thrown Union troops into panicked retreat through the tangled undergrowth and dense forests of western Virginia, an area known as the Wilderness.

The guards knew the Yankees were out there somewhere in the darkness, re-forming ranks. The fighting would begin again at first light—or before, if the enemy slipped past Confederate outposts and behind their lines. Suddenly, the sound of galloping horses brought the Rebels to full alert. Approaching horsemen emerged from the gloomy woods. There was no time to identify friend or foe in the confusion. A shot rang out. Then several more muzzles flashed, followed by volley of fire. No Yankees would pass this way.

Horses screamed and men shouted. The riders had been stopped in their tracks. But the guards had not shot Yankees—they had wounded ten Confederate officers. Then came the worst discovery of all—among the wounded was Stonewall Jackson himself. The great Rebel general had been shot three times.

Before the night was over, Jackson would lose his left arm. Within a week, Jackson would be dead, and Robert E. Lee would be without the man he called "his strong right arm." The general whose skills as a military leader had saved the lives of many men would die at the hands of those who needed him most.

Stonewall Jackson was mortally wounded by his own men in May 1863.

Chapter 1

FROM ORPHAN TO OFFICER

Nothing about Thomas "Stonewall" Jackson's early life indicated that he would become the most respected, loved-and-feared general of the Civil War. Thomas Jackson was born on January 21, 1824, in the small town of Clarksburg, Virginia, a region that became the state of West Virginia during the Civil War. His father, Jonathan Jackson, was a lawyer. He was a weak public speaker and a poor businessman, however, and the family was always in financial trouble.

OPPOSITE: Stonewall Jackson's childhood home near Weston, Lewis County, West Virginia, where he lived from age seven to age eighteen.

11

★

In 1826, when
Thomas was two,
Robert E. Lee was in
his second year at
West Point.

★

Thomas was the third child of Jonathan and Julia Jackson. When Thomas was two years old, typhoid fever struck his older sister. She died while her mother was pregnant with their fourth child. Even before the Jacksons could mourn her death, Jonathan Jackson caught the same disease and died. The next day, Julia gave birth to a daughter, Laura. Julia was now a widow with no money and three children: four year old Warren, two-year-old Thomas, and newborn Laura.

For several years, the small family lived in poverty. Julia worked as a teacher and sewed clothes for people in Clarksburg, but she never had enough money to do more than pay off debts still owed by Jonathan Jackson. Once, when Thomas and his brother walked through town without any shirts, a storekeeper asked them why they were only half-dressed. When they told him their mother was washing their only shirts, he took them in and gave each another shirt.

Julia remarried to a man who had even less money than she had. The family moved, but their luck did not change. Julia, who had been in poor health for years, became steadily worse. Warren was sent away to live with relatives. Though Julia was determined to keep Thomas and Laura with her, her illness left her too weak to provide for them. In the fall of 1831, the two youngest children were sent to live with relatives at a town called Jackson's Mill.

Later that year, Julia Jackson died. Her loss left Thomas an orphan, though he was fortunate to live with a family. He and Laura lived at Jackson's Mill for four years, until events forced the family to split the children up. Laura was placed with one set of relatives, while Thomas was sent to another.

By age twelve, Thomas had seen the deaths of several family members, had been separated from his brother and sister, and had moved between several households. As a result, he grew up with few social graces and felt uncomfortable in public. His wife would later write, "In his after years, he was not disposed to talk much of his childhood and youth, for the reason that it was the saddest period of his life."

★

In 1836, when Thomas was twelve, Abraham Lincoln was elected as a state representative in Illinois.

★

As difficult as it was, Thomas's childhood made him independent, self-sufficient, and direct. Relatives also noticed two characteristics that made him stand out— honesty and faith. While still living at Jackson's Mill, he had an arrangement with a local man, Mr. Kester, who agreed to pay Jackson fifty cents for every fish Thomas caught that was over a foot in length—a great deal of money in those days. One day, Thomas caught a three-foot pike. Several men who saw the fish tried to buy it, but Jackson refused to sell it to them, even at three times the usual price. He brought the fish to Mr. Kester, and refused to accept any more than the agreed fifty cents.

13

Thomas was also deeply devoted to his religion. As a teenager he often spoke of becoming a minister, and his faith stayed with him through the darkest periods of his life. This interest in religion led Thomas to pursue a formal education. He wanted to be able to read the Bible and other religious writings.

Thomas was not known as a great student, but he worked hard and teachers noticed his intensity. Facing a series of tasks, he would focus on only one, mastering that before moving to the next. A childhood friend said Thomas "was by no means . . . brilliant, but was one of those untiring, plain, matter-of-fact persons who would never give up . . . until he accomplished his object."

Thomas's favorite books were studies of famous battles, including the military campaigns described in the Bible. He was also fond of stories of Francis Marion, a hero of the American Revolution known as the "Swamp Fox," who was famous for his hit-and-run guerilla tactics. In later years, Thomas would use some of Marion's techniques in his own military campaigns.

Hard work outside of school was also a part of Thomas's daily life. At various times, he served as an engineering assistant, a teacher, and a constable. Although he worked hard at these jobs and did them well, none appealed to the young man as a career. When Thomas was eighteen, however, an opportunity arose that would change the course of his life.

Francis Marion, called the "Swamp Fox," was a hero of the American Revolution. Stonewall Jackson used many of Marion's "hit-and-run" tactics in his own battles.

Thomas learned that there was an opening for someone in his region to attend the United States Military Academy at West Point. He did everything possible to gain the appointment, which would give him both a free education and a military career. Unfortunately, Thomas's lack of social grace and his average education placed him second to another young man. Thomas was disappointed, but not for long. The other boy lasted less than a day at West Point before giving up and coming home. As soon as Thomas learned the position was re-opened, he arranged to be appointed.

West Point presented a great opportunity, but it also offered a huge challenge. Thomas was not prepared to compete with some of the nation's smartest and most privileged youth. A fellow cadet recorded Jackson's entrance exam. "His whole soul was bent on passing. When he went to the blackboard, the perspiration was streaming from his face, and during the whole examination his anxiety was painful to witness."

★

In 1846, British abolitionists purchased Frederick Douglass' "freedom" from his owner for $710.

★

Thomas barely passed the entrance exam, and he spent his first two years just trying to keep up with his classmates, a group that included twenty future Civil War generals. For those first years, Thomas was ranked near the bottom of the class.

By the time he graduated, however, he had moved up to seventeenth out of the fifty-nine graduates of 1846.

Some thought Thomas would have been at the top of his class if he had stayed at West Point for one more year. However, in 1846, the United States was at war with Mexico, and, with most of his classmates, Thomas was sent south to join the nation's army. Second Lieutenant Thomas Jackson was soon to have his first taste of war.

West Point
Class of 1846

★ ★ ★ ★ ★

Thomas Jackson graduated from West Point in 1846. In his time there, he rose from the bottom to almost the top quarter of his class. To achieve so much was remarkable, considering the quality of his classmates. Not only did many come from upper-class families, a number went on to achieve military distinction. Most of the class was sent to the war with Mexico immediately upon graduation.

General George Stoneman

Twenty of the fifty-nine graduates in 1846 would become generals in the Civil War, though none rose as high in achievement or respect as Jackson. In every major battle Jackson fought in the Civil War, he faced at least one former classmate, including his old roommate, George Stoneman, who commanded the Union cavalry during the campaign in which Jackson was killed. The class included George B. McClellan, whom Jackson faced in Virginia and at Antietam. It also included Confederate leader George E. Pickett, with whom Jackson served on the Virginia Peninsula and at Fredericksburg. Pickett later became famous for his "charge" at Gettysburg.

Chapter 2

SOLDIER AND TEACHER

Jackson's solid standing at West Point earned him a place with the First Artillery Regiment. He did not see any fighting in Mexico for several months, but when U.S. forces attacked the Mexican fortress at Vera Cruz on March 22, 1847, the new lieutenant experienced his first battle.

OPPOSITE: General Winfield Scott entering Mexico City, during the war with the United States.

Although it was not a full-scale battle, Jackson handled himself well during the fight. An officer who had been at school with Jackson watched him direct his artillery in the midst of the fighting. "Old Jack was as calm in the midst of a hurricane of bullets as though he were on dress parade at West Point," he reported.

Within five days, Vera Cruz surrendered. Commander of the U.S. forces, General Winfield Scott, pushed the army toward Mexico City. Days later, in a battle at Contreras, Jackson fought so bravely that he was promoted to First Lieutenant. Then, just outside Mexico City, at a castle called Chapultepec, Jackson showed the first real sign of military greatness.

> ★
>
> Jackson was strong enough to move a large artillery piece by himself.
>
> ★

Jackson's artillery was positioned at the far left of the American force. At one point, he pushed a cannon forward to protect a group of soldiers pinned down by Mexican guns. Gunfire was heavy and the horses used to move the artillery were killed. As his men prepared to retreat, Jackson stopped them, saying, "There is no danger! See? I am not hit!" Later, Jackson admitted this was the only lie he ever intentionally told—the Americans were indeed in great danger.

At that point in the battle, Jackson's squad was positioned ahead of the rest of the force, firing one gun while requesting reinforcements from the rear. Even when a general ordered him to fall back, Jackson delayed until help arrived. Some

20

credited Jackson's bravery with saving the battle for the Americans.

When Chapultepec fell, Scott immediately ordered an attack on Mexico City. Again, Jackson pushed his cannons ahead of the main army. This time, he was joined by Lieutenants Daniel Harvey Hill and Barnard Bee, both of whom would later become Confederate generals with Jackson. The 3 young officers with 50 men opposed a Mexican force of over 1,500, yet the American artillery forced the Mexicans to retreat.

Soon, the Mexican army had abandoned Mexico City, and word had spread through the U.S. army of Lieutenant Jackson's bravery. He became a hero. Jackson's deeds were mentioned in the report of almost every general in the fight, including General Scott. He was promoted to brevet major—a field promotion that did not mean an increase in pay or privilege, but was a way to honor a soldier for exceptional bravery. In only fifteen months, Jackson had become the fastest-rising U.S. officer in Mexico.

Jackson's unit remained in Mexico for almost a year after the last major battle was fought, as diplomats worked out a peace treaty. In July of 1848, he was transferred to New York, where he spent two years at Fort Hamilton. From there, he was assigned to Fort Meade, Florida.

By 1850, Jackson's military career had stalled. With no war to fight, there was little chance for

Virginia Military Institute, or VMI, was modeled after West Point. Jackson was a teacher there for ten years.

advancement. When he became involved in a series of disputes with a fellow officer, Jackson decided that his time as a soldier was over. In March of 1851, Jackson received an offer to become a professor at the Virginia Military Institute in Lexington. He resigned from the army in May, and began a new life.

Professor Jackson

Virginia Military Institute was a state college, modeled after West Point. Jackson taught science and artillery for a salary of $1,200 a year. He taught at VMI for ten years and was generally

considered one of the worst professors in the school. He was a boring speaker, and had no patience for students who refused to work as hard as he had at West Point.

Students had little respect for Jackson, calling him such nicknames as "Old Jack" and "Tom Fool." Some drew cartoons of Jackson on the classroom chalkboard, showing a man with enormous feet. Jackson's large shoe size had led to another nickname, "Square Box."

In his first year at VMI, Jackson argued with a student in one of his classes. He had the student, a senior, expelled from school for

23

disrespect. The angry student challenged Jackson to a duel, which the older man refused. That student, James Walker, later became General Walker and served under "Stonewall" Jackson in the Civil War.

Poor teacher or not, as time passed, students came to value Jackson's knowledge and honesty. Jokes about "Major" Jackson changed from ridicule to fondness.

Lexington became the only real home that Jackson knew as an adult. He became an active member of the Presbyterian Church and he even started a Sunday school for slaves and freedmen (former slaves). Jackson also gave up drinking, smoking, swearing, and gambling because he felt those actions went against his religious beliefs. He steadfastly considered Sunday to be a holy day when no work should be done. Because of this, he even avoided mailing letters near the end of the week to prevent them from traveling with mail carriers on Sunday, a day of rest.

Though Jackson was a part of Lexington society, he was never comfortable in social settings. At parties, he refused to eat or drink anything except his own bland dinner, and he was a stiff, awkward party guest. Still, in the autumn of 1852, he began to visit the daughter of a local minister. Eleanor Junkin fell in love with the tall, formal professor, and they were married on August 4, 1853. Jackson was twenty-nine, Ellie twenty-eight. The two moved into a spare room in the Junkins' Lexington house, and by winter, Ellie was pregnant.

Tragically, Jackson's happiness did not last. In October 1854, Ellie went into labor. The baby boy she had been carrying was born dead, and Eleanor began to bleed badly. An hour later, she too was dead. The joy of new life had become the sorrow of sudden death. Jackson, filled with grief, turned to his religion but found little comfort. "I do not see the purpose of God in this, the most bitter, trying affliction of my life, but I will try to be submissive though it breaks my heart."

Eventually, Jackson recovered from the terrible loss. In the summer of 1856, he traveled to Europe, and by the time he returned he appeared to be in good spirits for the first time since Eleanor's death. He was ready to find a new companion and began to court Mary Anna Morrison, a sister-in-law of his Mexican War friend, D. H. Hill. By early 1857, the two were engaged, and in July they married. Anna became pregnant on their honeymoon, and a daughter was born to them on April 30, 1858. Once again, however, Jackson's happiness did not last. The baby developed a liver disease, and no medicine could cure her. Mary Graham Jackson died on May 25. Once again, the cruel nature of life and death in the 1800s had broken Jackson's heart.

★

In 1856, abolitionist John Brown led raids against pro-slavery settlers in "Bleeding Kansas."

★

Chapter 3

During the time Jackson suffered personal tragedies, the United States headed steadily toward national tragedy. Disagreements between the North and the South had deepened. The two sides disagreed about slavery, about the role of the national government, about states' rights, and about numerous other political questions.

OPPOSITE: Conflicts between the North and South increased when John Brown led a group of abolitionists in an attack on the federal armory at Harpers Ferry. They were hoping to take weapons to arm slaves for a revolution, but Brown was captured and sentenced to death.

27

Jackson was split on many of the political issues. He was a Unionist and opposed the idea of states seceding if there was any other way to solve disputes. At the same time, he believed in the rights of states to govern themselves and was deeply loyal to his home state of Virginia. Jackson owned slaves, but he did not strongly defend the institution of slavery. Like many Americans, he hoped the two sides would find a compromise.

Unfortunately, the time for compromise had passed. The dispute between North and South widened in 1859 when group of abolitionists—opponents of slavery—led by John Brown of Kansas, attacked the federal armory at Harpers Ferry, Virginia. Brown hoped to capture weapons that could be used to arm slaves for a revolution. Instead, Brown's force was defeated, and one of his sons was killed.

Brown was captured and sentenced to death. Jackson and some VMI students were sent to observe the hanging. Also among the witnesses was young John Wilkes Booth. Jackson described the execution of the man whom many blamed for making matters worse between North and South:

> John Brown was hung today at about 11 1/2 A.M. He behaved with unflinching firmness . . . The sheriff placed the rope around his neck, threw a white cap over his head . . . the rope was cut by a single blow, & Brown fell through about 25 inches . . . after which the wind blew his lifeless body to & fro.

Brown's death did not stop the abolitionist movement or ease the tensions between North and South. In 1860, when Abraham Lincoln was elected president over strong Southern opposition, Jackson and many fellow Southerners knew in their hearts that the country was headed for war.

Abraham Lincoln's election increased the divide between North and South.

Jackson was still teaching at VMI when several Southern states, led by South Carolina, voted to secede and form the Confederate States of America. In Virginia, opinion was divided between Secessionists and Unionists. His sister Laura was a strong Unionist. Jackson, too, favored the Union, but only to a point. "In this country, there is a strong Union feeling . . . I am in favor of making a thorough trial for peace, and if we fail in this and the state is invaded to defend it with terrific resistance—even to taking no prisoners."

On April 12, 1861, that moderate position was no longer possible. In South Carolina, Confederate forces attacked Fort Sumter to drive the Union forces out. With that attack, the war had begun, and there was no more neutral

★
In 1861, Andrew Johnson became the only senator from a Southern state who refused to support the Confederacy.
★

29

position. At VMI, Jackson addressed a crowd of angry students. "The time for war has not yet come, but it will come and soon, and when it does come, my advice is to draw the sword and throw away the scabbard." On April 17, Virginia voted to secede.

Jackson greatly admired General Robert E. Lee.

Jackson's role in the new war was far from definite. Although he had been a decorated and respected officer in Mexico, he had been out of the army for ten years. When he retired from the army, his formal rank was first lieutenant, though he was a brevet major. Now, as a professor at a military college his first assignment was to march the cadets to Richmond, Virginia. There, men who knew of his deeds in Mexico

arranged to have him named colonel and
take command of the arsenal at Harpers
Ferry that had now fallen to the Confederacy.

Jackson was pleased to discover that
General Robert E. Lee was one of the top
Confederate military leaders. Lee had declined
Lincoln's offer to command the Union army,
deciding, like Jackson, to side with his beloved
home state of Virginia instead. Jackson had
known Lee in Mexico and considered him a
better leader than the Union's commanding
general, Winfield Scott.

Defending the Shenandoah

Harpers Ferry was an important town in the Civil
War. It was well north of Washington, located at a
point where Confederate and Union support
divided. The town of Harpers Ferry is in West
Virginia, which broke away from Virginia to
remain loyal to the Union and became a separate
state in 1863. The town was home to a federal
armory made famous by abolitionist John Brown's
raid in 1859. The town also protected the fertile
Shenandoah Valley, which Jackson considered his
home region, and which contained farms that
would supply Virginia and the entire Confederacy
with valuable food.

Surrounded by high cliffs on three sides, Harpers
Ferry was almost impossible to defend. The Union
forces assigned there had fled at the outbreak of
war, and now Jackson was sent to take command.

31

Lieutenant Alexander "Sandie" Pendleton was Stonewall Jackson's aid throughout the war.

At Harpers Ferry, Jackson began to gather companions who would surround him for the next two years. One was a surgeon, Doctor Hunter McGuire. Only twenty-five years old, McGuire would hardly leave Jackson's side from the day he arrived at the Ferry until Jackson's death. Lieutenant Alexander "Sandie" Pendleton served as Jackson's aide throughout the war. Another officer with him to the end was Major John Harman, who was the quartermaster and thus responsible for military supplies. Harman brought Jackson one of his most valued companions of the war: a horse, known to most as Little Sorrel.

Finally, at Harpers Ferry, Jackson met the charming, talented cavalry commander, James Ewell Brown (Jeb) Stuart. Though different in personality and fighting style, Jackson and Stuart became close friends.

Jackson served under the command of General Joseph Johnston, who did not favor holding Harpers Ferry. He thought the area was too

Jackson's Staff

★ ★ ★ ★ ★

Jackson formed his staff at Harpers Ferry in 1861. Many members stayed with him until his death. "Sandie" Pendleton was one of the youngest, and best known. Pendleton ran Jackson's headquarters from mid-1862 on with a firm hand. When faced with a tough question about any military detail, Jackson would often tell the questioner to ask Pendleton, because "if he doesn't know it, nobody does."

Henry Kyd Douglas was another well-known and well-liked member of Jackson's staff. Years later his book, *I Rode with Stonewall*, became one of the most popular books about the Civil War.

Jedediah Hotchkiss and J. K. Boswell were both engineers for Jackson, and Hotchkiss was one of the most highly-respected cartographers in the Confederacy. Quartermaster John Harman was responsible for keeping Jackson's army supplied, fed, and mobile. Harmon was famous for his rough language and crude style—so different from Jackson—but he moved wagons and mules as well as anyone. Finally, Hunter McGuire was the talented young surgeon who joined Jackson at Harpers Ferry and stayed with him until his death in 1863.

difficult to defend, especially for Jackson's untrained and untested volunteers. Johnston gave orders to remove all valuable equipment from the warehouses, destroy what was left, and leave the town to the Federals.

Though Jackson disagreed, he followed orders, and on June 14, 1861 explosions ripped through Harpers Ferry as the Confederates blew up the railroad bridge, the Shenandoah River bridge, and several arms-making buildings. Jackson's men withdrew to join the rest of Johnston's army.

Jackson had hoped for a fight. He had been drilling and training his men, and he had more faith in them than Johnston did. When told that Johnston thought a company of regular army were more valuable than an entire regiment of volunteers, Jackson responded, "The patriotic volunteer, fighting for his country and his rights, makes the most reliable soldier on earth."

Harpers Ferry, after Jackson's troops destroyed bridges and several buildings.

Less than a month after leaving Harpers Ferry, on July 2, Jackson fought his first battle since Mexico. Near the town of Falling Waters, his men met a larger Union force. Jackson's troops inflicted heavy casualties on the Union soldiers with few Confederate losses. For his achievement, Jackson was promoted to the rank of brigadier general.

Meanwhile, in eastern Virginia, Union General Irvin McDowell had been ordered to carry the war to the Confederate capital at Richmond. His first objective was the railroad crossing called Manassas Junction, near a stream called Bull Run. Controlling this junction would give the Union control of the major railroad lines between Washington and Richmond. Confederate General Pierre G. T. Beauregard was in command of the Southern forces near Manassas. As McDowell planned his attack, Beauregard learned from his scouts that he was outnumbered 33,000 to 22,000. He requested aid from General Joseph Johnston and his 11,000-man force of Confederates.

Jackson was reluctant to leave the Shenandoah Valley, but anxious to meet the Union in battle. As the time neared, Johnston proved the value of the railroads by moving troops rapidly east toward Manassas by train. There, assigned to protect the Confederate left side, Jackson was stationed near Henry House Hill. Beauregard planned to strike with his right side, which would place Jackson far from the main fight.

35

At 5:00 A.M. on Sunday, July 21, however, McDowell's men launched their own attack directly at Jackson's position. The first Confederates to meet the Federals were led by Generals Barnard Bee and Nathan Evans. Badly outnumbered, the Southerners fell back toward Henry House Hill.

Jackson knew that his position on the high ground was critical. If the Union captured the hill, they would be able to flank the Confederate army and crush them from the side. Though his men had never been in such a large battle, they were comforted by the confidence of Jackson. One soldier described the general's calm but iron-willed manner before the battle.

> The trust in God, and utter reliance on His will was surely there—but no apathetic calmness. The blaze of the eye . . . was unmistakable—there plainly was a soul on fire with deep feeling, and the ardor of battle. A slumbering volcano clearly burned beneath that face so calm and collected.

The battle raged into the afternoon as Union forces approached Henry House Hill, driving Bee and Evans' men before them. As one of Jackson's men later wrote, "The enemy were as thick as wheat in the field, and the long lines of blue could not be counted."

General Bee, whom Jackson had known at West Point and in Mexico, arrived at Jackson's position

36

with word that his men were in retreat. Jackson promised to hold the hill. With that, Bee returned to his disorganized and dispirited men. Pointing toward the figure of Jackson on the hill, Bee shouted, "Look men, there is Jackson standing like a stone wall! Rally behind the Virginians! Let us determine to die here, and we will conquer! Follow me!"

After Bull Run, Thomas Jackson was called "Stonewall" Jackson, and his troops were called the "Stonewall Brigade."

Bee did, in fact, die there that afternoon, but his men joined Jackson's and held the hill. From that point on, Thomas Jackson became "Stonewall" Jackson, and his hard-fighting troops were called the "Stonewall Brigade."

The battle lasted the rest of the day, but the Union soldiers were consistently turned back. By late afternoon the Federals began to break and flee back toward Washington. The battle had ended in a Union defeat with almost 3,000 soldiers killed, wounded and missing compared to fewer than 2,000 Confederate casualties. Jackson was disappointed that Johnston and Beauregard allowed the Union to retreat. He had learned the value of aggressively following up a victory in Mexico, and he wanted to apply it at Manassas. The commanding generals disagreed.

Chapter 4

"STONEWALL"

Jackson's men were proud of the role they had played at Manassas. One officer later wrote, "Our brigade is almost immortalized; but for us the day would have been lost."

"Old Jack," despite his odd habits and demanding ways, had proven to be an excellent battlefield leader. Still, his demands on his men were great, and they found that fame had not softened him at all.

OPPOSITE: Thomas "Stonewall" Jackson was known as an odd man and a tough commander, but he inspired great confidence in his troops.

39

In August, one of Jackson's officers learned that his wife had become seriously ill. When Jackson refused the man's request for emergency leave, the colonel came to ask him personally. "General, General, my wife is dying! I must see her!" Jackson responded by saying, "Man, do you love your wife more than your country?" The colonel resigned from the army, but he received news of his wife's death before he could arrange transport home.

If Jackson was tough on his men, he was equally hard on himself. Though he missed his wife terribly, he refused to take leave of his men to visit her. He wrote a constant stream of letters to her filled with affection and devotion. His own lonely boyhood and the tragedy of his first marriage made him particularly devoted to Anna, and that devotion had only deepened after the death of their child. When Anna asked him to visit her, he wrote,

> My darling, I can't be absent from my command, as my attention is necessary in preparing my troops for hard fighting should it be required; and as my officers and soldiers are not permitted to go and see their wives and families, I ought not to see my esposito (Spanish for 'little wife') as it might make the troops feel that they were badly treated.

By now, Jackson's heroism at Manassas had been widely reported, and in October "Stonewall" Jackson was promoted to major general. He continued to suggest aggressive moves against the

Union. Jackson was convinced that the South would have to carry the war into the North to force them to end the fighting. Few Confederate leaders were willing to take this drastic step. Most wanted to fight a defensive battle, hoping for aid from the European nations who relied on the South's cotton.

★

During the war, Union and Confederate control of the Shenandoah Valley would change hands more than fifty times.

★

Some Confederate leaders also felt that an invasion of Northern soil would go against what the rebellion stood for. For this reason, Jackson's statements were not well received by important figures such as General Johnston, Confederate Secretary of War Judah Benjamin, and Confederate President Jefferson Davis.

However, these powerful men came up with a way to use Jackson's aggression while removing him from the political region between Richmond and Washington. In late October 1861, Jackson was assigned control of the Shenandoah Valley and the area west. Western Virginia had strong Union ties, and Federal troops were free to threaten the crucial valley from there.

Jackson's aggression, it was hoped, would protect this area. The news brought a mixed reaction from Jackson. The distance gave him some independence in command, though he was still under Johnston's overall control. But moving west meant he would have to leave his battle-toughened Stonewall Brigade and train a new force. On the day he left, he addressed his men.

41

Jackson's own wife Anna had arrived the month before. One officer wrote home, "If ever Genl. Jackson & I change places, I will send him to do duty in the summer time in Mississippi positively forbidding him to visit his wife."

On December 27, Loring and his last men finally joined Jackson at Winchester. At 9:00 A.M. on New Year's Day, 1862, Jackson began his campaign. The temperature dropped as the men marched, and the next day, snow began to fall. There were very few major campaigns planned during winter in the Civil War, because of roads and weather. Even if men could walk on snow, ice, or mud-covered roads, the wagons they relied on for supplies were too heavy.

★
In January 1862, a Union victory at Mill Springs, Kentucky, gave control of eastern Tennessee to Federal forces.
★

On January 4, Jackson's men defeated Union soldiers in a small skirmish at the town of Bath. The next day, his men destroyed part of the B&O Railroad and a bridge, cutting the Union's western forces supply lines from Washington. The mission was accomplished in heavy snow and bitter cold. Horses without winter shoes slipped, injuring riders and damaging supplies. Men with thin uniforms and worn shoes dropped from the ranks, and wagons sunk in the muddy trails.

The tattered forces were in luck, however, because, scouts returned to Jackson with news that the Union had abandoned Romney. Hearing of the defeat at Bath, they had exaggerated the size of Jackson's force and fled in fear. Jackson

44

marched his men to the town to take over the abandoned Union supplies. The march was as difficult as any, but many of the men still respected their leader even if they questioned some of his demands. One member of the Stonewall Brigade described the march:

Private John Rhodes of the Stonewall Brigade

Muddy roads and many streams to cross. At every step some one cursing 'old Jackson' for taking us on such a march at such a time and in such weather. In the midst of the cursing and grumbling, along rides our general on Old Sorrel. Immediately the cursing stops, and all with one accord begin to cheer. He gallops by, his cap in hand and eyes to the front . . . Though the march was hard and toilsome, we felt that he knew what he was doing and that it was best for us.

From Romney, Jackson hoped to continue to the Cumberland Gap and regain western Virginia, while controlling the most important path between the east and the west. When Confederate leaders did not supply him with the troops he requested, he gave up his plan. He made plans for winter quarters, leaving Loring's men in Romney while he returned to Winchester with the Stonewall Brigade.

One of the most common complaints about Stonewall Jackson as a leader was his complete refusal to share information. He had always valued secrecy, telling his officers only what he thought they needed to know. Given the number of times he was outnumbered and almost trapped during the Civil War, this made sense. He could not take a chance on having an officer captured and perhaps forced to reveal key information.

To his officers, however, it sometimes appeared that Jackson did not trust them. General Loring was particularly angered by this policy after being left in Romney. If something should happen to Stonewall, no one knew what the army's mission was. Loring and his men complained to Richmond about their position and eventually Secretary of War Benjamin ordered Loring's men to move to Winchester. This was done with President Davis's approval. Jackson's anger was obvious as he sent his response: "With such interference in my command I cannot expect to be of much service in the field . . . I respectfully request that the President will accept my resignation from the Army." The people of Winchester and the Stonewall Brigade were furious, and according to one witness, Jackson "was the only calm and unexcited man among us."

Jackson's request was not an empty threat. He honestly believed that he could not operate with interference from Richmond, and he could not succeed unless the Confederate leaders had great confidence in him. In Richmond, powerful friends of Jackson took up the issue. Davis and Benjamin both sensed they had overstepped their role, and sent Jackson's friends back to ask him to withdraw his resignation.

By early February, Jackson agreed. General Loring was ordered to southern Virginia, and Jackson's control over the Valley was confirmed. Unfortunately, Loring's abandonment of Romney allowed the Union to return to the town, rebuilding bridges, canals, and railroads that Jackson had damaged. With Union soldiers again threatening Winchester, the Confederacy had nothing to show for Jackson's winter campaign.

Change of Fortune

By late winter, two large Union armies near the Shenandoah threatened Jackson's force of 6,000. Union General Nathaniel Banks commanded 38,000 men and another Union army under General John C. Fremont waited in the Allegheny Mountains with close to 12,000 men. In late February, Banks brought his large force across the Potomac at Harpers Ferry and slowly made his way to Winchester. Jackson decided against fighting there, and withdrew south into the Valley. He sent his wife to live with relatives in Farmville, Virginia. His concern for her was increased by the knowledge that she was pregnant again.

★

In early 1862, General Robert E. Lee was in charge of coastal defenses in South Carolina, Georgia, and Florida.

★

47

Union victories in Tennessee led Lincoln to appoint Andrew Johnson the military governor of the state.

★

Jackson's troops gained some soldiers as they marched away from Winchester when local militiamen joined the force. One man, in particular, became valuable to Jackson. Jedediah Hotchkiss, whom Jackson had met once in Lexington, was an engineer, a schoolteacher, and most importantly, a cartographer, or mapmaker. He knew the Valley as well as anyone, and Jackson assigned him the job of mapping the region.

In Washington, President Lincoln was restless and unhappy with the lack of progress of the war in the East. The Union had achieved some success in North Carolina and in Tennessee at Forts Henry and Donelson, which led to the Federal capture of Nashville. Most advisors, however, told Lincoln that the key to defeating the Confederacy was capturing Richmond. The president ordered General George McClellan to attack the Southern capital, and McClellan chose to attack from the Virginia peninsula south of Richmond.

McClellan decided that Jackson was not a real threat, and he ordered Banks to move two of his three Union divisions toward Manassas, leaving General James Shields in the Shenandoah Valley with one division of 10,000 men. Jackson knew that Banks' move toward Manassas could eventually allow the Union to surround Richmond. He decided to act immediately to gain Banks' attention.

Pushing his men quickly north on March 22, Jackson began the first of many famous marches in his career. His soldiers would proudly earn the name "foot cavalry" for the distance and speed they could march. One soldier later described that trek: "We made a forced march . . . that resulted in aching limbs, sore feet, empty stomachs . . . For one day and a half we marched as only Jackson's men could march."

Covering more than twenty miles that day, Jackson prepared to attack Shields. He had been informed by his cavalry commander, Turner Ashby, that most of the Union army had departed leaving only about 1,000 men to oppose Jackson. Despite losing many men along the road during the hard march, Jackson had over 3,000 troops ready to fight.

★

In March 1862, General Robert E. Lee was ordered to Richmond to serve as personal advisor to Jefferson Davis.

★

The next day, Jackson encountered Shields' men near Kernstown, just south of Winchester. He ordered the attack to begin, but, as usual, he did not tell his officers the details of his plans, preferring to command the battle himself. As more Union forces appeared, Jackson became worried. He sent his aide, Sandie Pendleton, to check on the Union strength. Pendleton returned with the news that the Union had nearly 10,000 men. "Say nothing about it," said Jackson, "We are in for it."

Jackson's outnumbered men fought hard, but eventually his refusal to involve his officers in command decisions backfired. General Richard Garnett, who commanded the Stonewall Brigade, was in the center of the Confederate line.

Convinced that his men could not hold their position, Garnett chose to withdraw. This exposed the Confederates on his left, who were suddenly flanked by advancing Union troops. The entire Confederate line collapsed and had to retreat.

Kernstown was Jackson's only defeat in the Civil War. He lost 718 men, while the Union lost 590. In the long run, however, Kernstown proved to be an important Confederate victory. Union leaders could not believe Stonewall Jackson would attack such a large force unless his own numbers were much higher than the Union thought. Therefore, Union General Banks was ordered to turn his men around and march back to the Valley, away from Richmond. In addition, another division was removed from McClellan's command and sent to join Fremont in the west, while an entire corps was kept at Manassas. In all, Jackson's move probably kept 60,000 Union men from joining McClellan's attack on Richmond.

Jackson also made clear how he felt about officers who acted without orders. General Garnett had not known the consequences of his withdrawal because Jackson had never explained his full strategy. Still, Jackson expected Garnett and all his men to hold their positions until ordered to move. Jackson had General Garnett arrested to await a court-martial. That court-martial would never be completed, but it created great tension within the Stonewall Brigade. Though his career was permanently

50

damaged by Jackson's charges, General Garnett would later say at Jackson's funeral, "No one can lament (regret) his death more sincerely than I do. I believe that he did me a great injustice, but I believe also that he acted from the purest motives."

Jackson's Foot Cavalry

By spring 1862, Robert E. Lee began to have more influence in Richmond, as President Davis's military advisor. While Johnston was opposing McClellan on the Yorktown peninsula, Lee began to deal more closely with Jackson. Hoping that Jackson's aggressive moves could reduce the threat to Richmond even more, Lee encouraged Jackson. The strong bond that developed between these two men would shape the course of Civil War for the following year.

Union General Nathaniel Banks

Lee did not need to give Jackson much encouragement to take the offensive. He was not concerned by the fact that he was still badly outnumbered. With his 8,500 men in the Valley, plus another 8,500 Rebels under General Richard Ewell, Jackson faced 19,000 troops to his north under Banks and another 20,000 to the west under Fremont. As spring warmed the region, the two Union forces moved toward Jackson.

Jackson decided to hit Fremont first. He left Ewell in front of Banks—without telling Ewell his

51

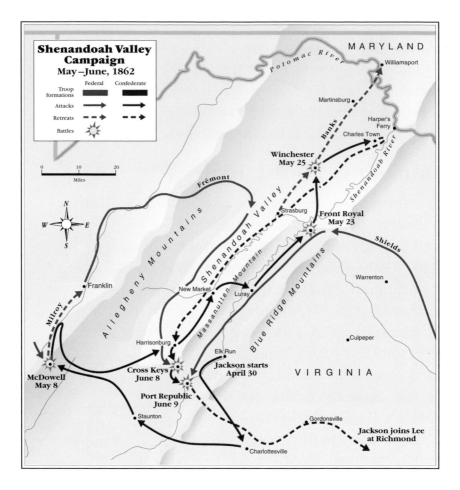

whole plan. Then Jackson marched his men east, to confuse Banks. The plan worked. On April 28, Banks wrote to Washington, "Our force is entirely secure here. The enemy is in no condition for offensive movement," and later, added, "Jackson is bound for Richmond. That is the fact, I have no doubt." In fact, once he was away, Jackson secretly circled around to the west, where his men confronted Fremont's lead forces and defeated them on May 8.

Jackson then sent Jedediah Hotchkiss to block all three mountain passes between Fremont and Banks. Rolling boulders, chopping trees, and burning bridges, Hotchkiss and his group of soldiers blocked the passes and kept the Union army from uniting.

In April 1862, Union forces under Grant won a costly victory at Shiloh in Tennessee.

With Fremont's main force closed off, Jackson turned his attention to General Banks. He had assigned Ewell to watch the movement of Banks' force. But Jackson had not told Ewell what was planned or what Ewell was expected to do. This secrecy, especially toward a major general who was equal in rank to Jackson, made Ewell furious. At one point, he exploded to one of his officers, "I tell you, sir, he is as crazy as a March hare! He has gone away, I don't know where, and left me here with some instructions to stay until he returns, but . . . I haven't the most remote idea where to communicate with General Jackson! I tell you, sir, he is crazy!" Later, Ewell added, "This man Jackson is certainly a crazy fool, an idiot!"

What Ewell did not know was that Jackson was circling around behind Banks. The Union commander, believing he was in no danger, had sent one of his divisions out of the valley. Jackson planned to unite with Ewell and destroy Banks and his Federals.

With over 16,000 men, Jackson faced a Union force that was thinly spread out. Banks had some 6,000 men with him at Strasburg, 1,500 at Front

53

Royal, and another 1,500 at Winchester. Jackson's first target was the town of Front Royal. By May 22, Jackson's men had marched 120 miles in 10 days—almost completely undetected. In a time when armies often moved only a few miles in a given day and were challenged to move 80 miles in a week, Jackson set a new standard.

His "foot cavalry," the most mobile foot soldiers in the Civil War, were beginning to build a remarkable reputation.

On May 23, Jackson's men attacked Front Royal. The attack came as a surprise to the Union soldiers, who were quickly overrun. Though the fighting for a while was fierce, Jackson's troops captured more

This illustration, from Frank Leslie's *Illustrated Newspaper*, shows Stonewall Jackson's army fighting a battle in the Shenandoah Valley.

than 700 Union soldiers and tons of supplies while losing less than 100 soldiers. Hearing of the loss, Banks ordered his Strasburg troops to pull back to Winchester on May 24.

Jackson pushed his men to follow. He wanted to control the hills around Winchester before the next morning, which meant marching through the night. Some soldiers recalled that as the worst night of their lives—many actually slept as they marched. One officer protested to Jackson, begging for a rest for his men. Jackson responded, "Colonel, I yield to no man in my sympathy for the gallant men under my command; but I am obliged to sweat them tonight that I may save their blood tomorrow."

He knew that he had to put his guns on the hills before Banks could do so.

★
Soldiers who fell behind during Jackson's marches were called "stragglers."
★

At 4:00 on the morning of May 25, Jackson's 10,000 men—many had been lost to exhaustion—attacked Banks and his 6,500 Union soldiers. By 8:30 A.M. the Union was in retreat. The fight at Winchester had cost the Union over 3,000 men compared to only 400 Confederate casualties. Jackson had also captured an enormous store of weapons, food, ammunition, and medical supplies. Several Union doctors stayed with their wounded in Winchester. Jackson allowed them to finish their work and return to the North rather than making them prisoners of war.

Men on both sides of the war were astounded by Jackson's success. One Confederate soldier declared,

55

"I'd rather be a private under Jackson than an officer in another army." Richmond newspapers called him a "man of high military genius . . . very daring . . . Jackson has shown what a brave heart and ready wit can do . . . Men will follow such a leader anywhere."

On the Union side, a shocked President Lincoln ordered McClellan to either begin his action against Richmond or return to defend Washington. He stopped Union General Irvin McDowell from leaving Fredericksburg to aid McClellan, and ordered Banks' brigade and 15,000 more soldiers to enter the valley. He also ordered General Fremont into action. The Union was determined to defeat the famous Stonewall Jackson.

Victory in the Valley

Now Jackson was the one in danger. With Banks to his north at Harpers Ferry, Fremont coming from the southwest, and McDowell's two divisions approaching from the east, Jackson seemed to be trapped. On May 30, Jackson learned that a Union force had re-taken Front Royal. With Fremont's approach, this meant 35,000 Union soldiers, more than twice what Jackson had, were in position to cut off Jackson's escape and could trap him. As General Shields wrote to General Fremont, "I hope you will thunder down on his rear . . . I think Jackson is caught this time."

At 3:00 A.M. on May 31, Jackson began moving his troops south to escape the Union trap. They marched fifty minutes in every hour, stopping only for ten-minute breaks. When the Confederates reached Strasburg, Jackson's foot cavalry had marched close to forty miles in two days in pouring rain and without food. It was a remarkable effort, which saved many lives. One soldier joked that Jackson was a better leader than Moses. When asked why, the man responded, "It took Moses forty years to lead the Israelites through the Wilderness, while Jackson would have double-quicked them through in three days."

Jackson was aiming for the tiny town of Port Republic. This was the point at which the two forks of the Shenandoah River came together and the last place where he could keep Fremont and Shields from joining forces against him. By June 5, most of his troops had marched 104 miles in 7 days in mud and rain without rest and with very little food. The terrible pace had cost Jackson as much as twenty percent of his forces, lost to illness and exhaustion. On June 6, Jackson placed his own men around Port Republic, while Ewell's men were stationed at nearby Cross Keys to watch Fremont's approach. Late that day, Jackson received news that his cavalry commander, Turner Ashby, had been killed in a skirmish near Harrisonburg.

★
Jackson called soldiers who fell by the wayside during a march "unpatriotic."
★

On the morning of June 8, a Federal cavalry regiment attacked Port Republic. With Ashby's death, Jackson had no reliable cavalry leader to maintain a line of scouts, and the arrival of the

Union soldiers came as a surprise. Jackson himself was almost captured—two of his staff became prisoners—before he turned the attack away. At the same time, Fremont launched an attack on Ewell at Cross Keys.

Richard Ewell held his ground successfully, despite being badly outnumbered. Fremont's 10,500 men could not push Ewell's 5,000 troops back. The Union actually lost ground and suffered more than twice as many casualties as the Confederates. The next day, Jackson ordered part of Ewell's force to hold off Fremont, while Jackson himself led the attack against General Shields. Ewell was so impressed with Jackson's plans at this point that he reversed his earlier opinions. "I take it all back," he said, "I will never prejudge another man. Old Jackson's no fool. He has a method in his madness."

The battle started poorly for Jackson, who had trouble getting all his men across the river to meet Shields. By mid-morning he ordered the rest of Ewell's men to withdraw from engagement with Fremont's force, cross the river to Jackson's side, and burn the bridge behind them. With particular bravery from the Stonewall Brigade, Jackson was able to hold his position until more help arrived. By midday, the Union line had broken. Shields had lost over 1,000 men, to Jackson's 800, but the impact of Port Republic was greater than that. As Jackson pulled back, Shields' men were in retreat and Fremont's men could only watch from the other side

Stonewall Jackson

of the burned bridge. The next day, both battered Union forces moved away from Jackson's army.

This marked the end of the valley campaign. Though he made some mistakes along the way, Stonewall Jackson had accomplished a remarkable overall victory. With 17,000 men, he held off and defeated almost 60,000 Union soldiers. He had inflicted over 6,000 casualties while losing fewer than 3,000 himself. More importantly, he kept vital Union troops away from the attack on Richmond, which changed the North's strategies. Finally, he gave the South pride and confidence at a point when their cause appeared lost. Jackson's work in the valley has been considered among the finest military campaigns in history.

A soldier in Richmond wrote home, "All eyes now seem to be centered on General T. J. Jackson . . . I am fully convinced that he is the only General on either side in this War who shows any of that genius which is necessary to the managing of armies."

Wounded and ragged soldiers of General Fremont's army, marching through the Shenandoah Valley.

Chapter 5

JACKSON AND LEE

Despite the thousands of soldiers occupied by Jackson's maneuvers in the Shenandoah Valley, George McClellan still had over 100,000 Federal troops on the Virginia peninsula, south of Richmond. In a battle there, known as Seven Pines, on May 31, Confederate General Joseph Johnston was wounded and was replaced by Robert E. Lee. Up to this point, Lee had not been in command of an army in the field. Few people knew, in fact, that it was Lee's overall plan that Jackson followed in the Shenandoah to occupy the Federal forces. Though Lee's excellence as a commander was not yet known to many in the Confederacy, Jackson already had a high opinion of him. Jackson once said, "So great is my confidence in General Lee that I am willing to follow him blindfolded."

OPPOSITE: The Union lost almost 7,000 men, and the Confederates lost nearly 9,000, at the Battle of Gaines Mill.

Lee was equally impressed with Jackson. Stonewall's combination of daring and drive had earned him great praise and respect, and now Lee decided that the defense of Richmond required the help of this remarkable leader. Jackson and his troops were ordered to proceed at once to Richmond. Again, Jackson's focus on secrecy angered his officers, but worked effectively with the enemy. Long after Jackson's men had left the valley, the Union troops still believed "Old Stonewall" might attack them at any moment.

On June 23, an exhausted Jackson met with Lee outside Richmond. Generals James Longstreet and Ambrose Powell Hill were there, as was Jackson's old friend, D. H. Hill. Lee outlined his plan to push George McClellan off the peninsula. Jackson would drive his men south toward Richmond, on A. P. Hill's left. Longstreet would support A. P. Hill, while D. H. Hill would support Jackson. The other commanders all knew the area, Jackson did not. In addition, Jackson was physically and emotionally exhausted. His men were no better off.

★

Early in the war, Southern newspapers called Lee "Granny Lee" while accusing him of being reluctant to fight.

★

Jackson's weariness might explain why he couldn't move his men as quickly as he needed to, and his ignorance of the region meant that he didn't realize how far his men had to march. In the valley, Jackson had his mapmaker, Hotchkiss, describe regions to him. Hotchkiss was of no help in the territory around Richmond.

The Seven Days

Jackson's march was delayed on June 25th and 26th. By morning on the 26th, he was a full six hours behind schedule, and other Confederate leaders had lost contact with each other. When A. P. Hill attacked without hearing from the others, Jackson was not in position to help, and the Yankees were able to put all their men against Hill. Even when Jackson did arrive within sound of the guns, he had no orders to fight, so he held his position. A. P. Hill's men were slaughtered, as the Confederates lost over 1,400 men to fewer than 400 for the Union.

That night, the Federal soldiers moved to Gaines Mill where they set up new defenses. On June 27, the fight again went against the Confederate plans. Union troops were not where they were thought to be, and Jackson's men lost valuable time. By the time Jackson joined the fight at Gaines Mill, the rest of the Confederate army was almost defeated. However, Jackson's arrival was like a heavenly sign. His power to inspire soldiers was growing almost daily. One of Longstreet's soldiers later wrote,

Could it be true? A deafening shout burst from our men; thousands of throats took it up and rent the very air; it died away only to be repeated in greater emphasis and volume. The news ran along the lines like an electric flash . . . Stonewall Jackson here!

A Confederate cannon in position at the James River, 1862.

Jackson shook off his weariness and led his men into the battle. Together, the Confederate forces were able to carry the day, but at high cost. The Union lost almost 7,000 men compared to the Confederates' losses of nearly 9,000, but the Union withdrawal marked the fight at Gaines Mill as a Confederate victory. McClellan began to move his forces away from Richmond toward the James River.

Stonewall Jackson was assigned to chase McClellan while Lee tried to get around in front of the Union with the rest of the army. On June 30, Union soldiers and artillery held their ground against Jackson at White Oak Swamp. At the same time, Longstreet, A. P. Hill, and Lee were not able to halt the Union movement, and McClellan brought his troops together at Malvern Hill.

Lee spent the night of June 30 and the next morning gathering his own forces. By noon, close to 80,000 Confederates faced the same number of

Stonewall Jackson

Federal soldiers. Since Jackson's men had fought least the day before, they led the assault on Malvern Hill. But the strong Union positions proved to be unbreakable, as the Confederates found out. D. H. Hill, who lost many men in those assaults, later said, "My recollections of Malvern Hill are so unpleasant that I do not like to write about it. Twas a mistake to fight."

That battle ended the fighting called the Seven Days Campaign. McClellan fell back that night to his waiting gunboats on the James River, and showed no sign of leaving their protection. The Seven Days had pushed the Union back from the gates of Richmond to the edge of the peninsula, at great cost to both sides. McClellan lost almost 16,000 men, while Lee lost more than 20,000. Though successful in saving Richmond, neither Jackson nor Lee had proved effective leaders in the battles. Lee, new to this level of field command, did not communicate or coordinate attacks well. Jackson, unfamiliar with the area and too tired to use good judgement, was consistently late and hesitant in his movements.

★
Union forces on the peninsula lost more men to diseases such as typhoid fever and malaria than in battle.
★

West Again

By early July, Lee's attention was focused back on the Shenandoah Valley. President Lincoln had decided to unite the Federal forces in the region under General John Pope, who had given the Union some victories along the Mississippi River. Pope

General John Pope was appointed by President Lincoln to unite and command all Federal forces.

quickly made himself unpopular with both sides. He angered Union soldiers under his command by suggesting that the valley forces had not fought hard against Jackson in the winter and spring.

To infuriate Southerners, Pope promised to confiscate and destroy Southern property, imprison civilians, and shoot captured "guerrilla" fighters. The logical choice to meet this new threat was the hero of the Shenandoah, Stonewall Jackson.

This time, however, Jackson was much less independent. Lee had reorganized the Army of Northern Virginia, as his force was now called. He broke the entire infantry into two large commands under Jackson and Longstreet. Jackson's command was made up of his old division now under General Charles Winder, Richard Ewell's division, and A. P. Hill's division. The other four infantry divisions were under Longstreet, and all of the cavalry were put under the command of Jackson's friend, Jeb Stuart. Although this elevated Jackson's position in the army, it meant that he would be much more closely tied to Lee and to Longstreet, and could no longer operate on his own.

Pope had taken over and united the commands of Banks, Fremont, and McDowell. He had placed himself at Culpeper, Virginia, where he could threaten the only direct railroad link between Richmond and the Shenandoah Valley. By early August 1862, Jackson had brought his corps of 22,000 Rebels to Gordonsville, along the valuable railroad line. Pope's 50,000 Federals were stretched out in a line 30 miles to Jackson's north. In addition, another 11,000 Federals were stationed 40 miles east of Jackson at Fredericksburg. In early August, McClellan was ordered to abandon the peninsula and move his troops north to Fredericksburg. From there, the Union general could both defend Washington and threaten Richmond. On August 7, Jackson moved his troops north to Orange Court House, then, on August 9, he moved his army to engage Pope's Federals.

At Cedar Mountain, just south of Culpeper, Jackson encountered 12,000 Union soldiers under his old Valley enemy, General Banks. After an artillery duel in summer heat so brutal that several men died from heat stroke, Banks ordered his

This engraving shows Fredericksburg after Union troops ransacked it in late 1862.

infantry to attack. This sudden attack by the outnumbered Federal troops took the Confederates by surprise, and disaster loomed when General Winder was fatally shot. The Union had found a seam between the two Confederate units and threatened to destroy Jackson's command.

At the bleakest point, Stonewall Jackson took action himself. Grabbing his sword, which he had never used in battle and was rusted into the sheath, in one hand, and a Confederate battle flag in the other, he waved both to gain the attention of his battered troops. With bullets flying around him, he shouted, "Rally, brave men, and press forward! Your general will lead you! Jackson will lead you! Follow me!" His men responded. One officer later wrote, "The men would have followed him into the jaws of death itself."

Though Jackson was convinced to withdraw to relative safety after rallying the troops, there is no question he helped hold his men together. Still, the day might have been lost if A. P. Hill had not arrived with much-needed reinforcements. At that point, the Confederates were able to push the Union soldiers from the field. In the end, the battle was a victory for Jackson, with 2,500 Union casualties compared to 1,400 Confederates, but it had almost been a disaster.

Back to Manassas

After Cedar Mountain, Jackson hoped to follow his victory by crushing Banks on his retreat. However,

General Pope called up fresh Union troops to support Banks and stop Jackson's advance. Now facing an overwhelming force, Jackson withdrew to Gordonsville. There, on August 15, he was joined by Robert E. Lee and James Longstreet. Together, they formed a daring plan.

While Lee and Longstreet kept Pope's attention to the south, Jackson would march his men in a loop around Pope's entire army, and attack the Orange and Alexandria Railroad behind him. This would cut Union communications, and when Pope turned to attack Jackson, Lee and Longstreet could attack from his rear. Pope would be trapped.

The plan was dangerous. If McClellan's men arrived while the Confederates were divided, they could crush the smaller Southern forces. Also, Jackson would be badly outnumbered by Pope if Lee didn't attack quickly enough. Finally, Jackson would have to move his men over fifty miles in great speed and secrecy for the plan to succeed. This was exactly what Jackson's "foot cavalry" had been training for throughout the war, and they were up to the task.

At 3:00 A.M. on August 25th, Jackson's three divisions began their march. Jackson led his 23,000 soldiers in complete secrecy—only he and a single scout knew where they were going. Jackson allowed no breaks on the march—the men ate as they walked. By nightfall, they had covered twenty-six miles. Even Stonewall Jackson, who consistently demanded great efforts from his men, was pleased.

69

He turned to an officer and proudly asked, "Who could not conquer with such troops as these?"

The march began again in the middle of the night. Their destination was Bristoe Station, and the Orange and Alexandria Railroad bridge there. Arriving by nightfall, Jackson's men scattered a group of Federal soldiers and destroyed the rails, forcing two trains to wreck. Unfortunately for the Confederates, a third train escaped to Manassas Junction up the line and another was able to reverse its course back to Warrenton. This meant the Union knew Jackson's location.

The "foot cavalry" had accomplished an almost impossible mission. In less than two days, they had covered fifty-six miles in secrecy, swung around behind Pope's huge force, and partially destroyed a main railroad connection. Still, Jackson had one more goal to accomplish. He heard of a massive Union supply depot at Manassas Junction, where he had earned his nickname a year before.

The scene at Manassas, Virginia, after retreating Confederates destroyed the Orange and Alexandria railroad lines.

Since Pope's army was more than double Jackson's size, the Union general believed he could finally crush his enemy. But Jackson wanted Pope to attack him in order to distract the Union from their flank. Pope did not know of Longstreet's 31,000 Confederates marching to surprise him. At 6:00 P.M. on August 28, Jackson ordered an attack on a Federal brigade under Union General John Gibbons. Gibbon's brigade would soon earn the nickname "Iron Brigade" and become one of the Union's most feared fighting forces. As the Stonewall Brigade fought the Iron Brigade, two of the proudest groups of soldiers in the Civil War opposed each other. Though the Confederates eventually pushed Gibbons' men back, both sides took heavy casualties. The South lost General Taliaferro and General Ewell to serious wounds. Though both would survive, Jackson was without their services for the rest of the battle.

The fight told Pope exactly where to find Jackson, which was part of the wily Confederate general's plan. That night, the rebels took up positions for the clash ahead. They hoped for the arrival of Longstreet, but until help arrived, Jackson had only about 18,000 healthy men on the line. Pope's entire force numbered over 60,000.

At 10:00 A.M. on August 29, the fight began, with the Confederates behind an unfinished railroad embankment. The Union numbers began to press the Confederates, forcing a hole in Jackson's line.

★
Throughout 1862, Frederick Douglass traveled through Northern states, speaking out for African Americans to be allowed to enlist.
★

71

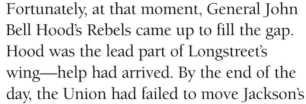
Fortunately, at that moment, General John Bell Hood's Rebels came up to fill the gap. Hood was the lead part of Longstreet's wing—help had arrived. By the end of the day, the Union had failed to move Jackson's men, and Pope still did not know he faced the entire Army of Northern Virginia, over 50,000 men strong.

The next day began quietly. On the Union side, men were unsure of Pope's intention. As one soldier commented, "We spent the first half of the day in marching back and forth in an aimless sort of way, occasionally halting as if waiting for some one to put us on the right road."

At 3:00 that afternoon, the Federals finally began their attack, expecting to find that Jackson had pulled back in the night. The Federals crashed into Jackson's position. Wave after wave of the Union soldiers drove into the Confederates as Lee held Longstreet's men back. Finally, Longstreet's artillery opened fire on the Federal left flank. Then, 25,000 fresh Confederate troops poured into the fight. In the words of a Northern observer, the Rebels "came on, like demons emerging from the earth." The Union men were in full retreat.

The Confederates had lost over 9,000 men. The Union, however, lost over 16,000 men, and the damage to their pride and spirit could not be measured. Most of the blame for the defeat was placed on the head of General Pope. As one Union officer wrote, "So long as the interests of our country are entrusted to a lying braggart like

Jackson's troops, like many Confederates, were often short on supplies. In some battles, they were forced to fight with stones or even their bare hands.

Pope, we have little reason to hope successfully to compete with an army led by Lee, Johnston, and old 'Stonewall" Jackson." In less than a week, John Pope had been sent to Minnesota to fight Indians, far from any important battleground. At the same time, Stonewall Jackson had become the most respected and feared leader in the war. While Southern newspapers praised him so highly that Jackson refused to read them, the North trembled at the mention of his name. One Union soldier reported, "The greatest horror is entertained of Jackson whom they seem to regard as a species of demon."

"Old Jack's" Ailments

★ ★ ★ ★ ★

One thing that made Thomas Jackson seem odd to his companions was his constant list of ailments—and his strange remedies. Though some of Jackson's illnesses were very real, it is also true that they only seemed to bother him when things were quiet. At the height of his military campaigns he almost never expressed any discomfort or fear of illness. Between campaigns and in peacetime, his letters were full of complaints and concerns for his health. At various points, he wrote of his poor eyesight, hearing, throat, digestion, liver, kidneys, blood circulation, nervous system, muscles, and joints. Among the diseases he claimed to have were rheumatism (painful joints), neuralgia (pain along the nerves), and dyspepsia (severe indigestion).

Taking the War North

From the beginning, Jackson believed that the only way the Union would end its fight was if they were convinced of the South's determination. He had tried to convince Confederate leaders to invade the North after the First Battle of Bull Run, and he had requested permission to invade more than once

To combat these problems, Jackson followed a unique system of treatment. He regularly exercised, including aerobic and calisthenic exercises, which were not yet popular. He also tried all sorts of "wonder medicines" recommended to him. He believed strongly in "water treatments" or hydrotherapy, which involved use of spas and mineral springs. Finally, to combat his chronic indigestion, he developed his own odd diet. It included stale bread, plain meat (broiled or roasted), egg yolks, black tea, one vegetable per dinner, and fresh fruit. His fondness for peaches was well known.

To protect his fragile health when invited to dinner, he would either refuse to eat his host's food or would bring his own. During the war, his staff quickly grabbed most gifts of food that poured in, since they knew Jackson would only send them back.

while in the Shenandoah Valley. Finally, after the Second Battle of Bull Run, he had his chance.

With Pope disgraced and his western force broken, President Lincoln recalled McClellan to Washington. The Union feared a Confederate attack on the capital, but Lee knew it was too well defended. He wanted to invade the North and force a fight on ground he chose, so he aimed for Hagerstown in western Maryland. From there, according to his plan he would push on to Harrisburg, Pennsylvania. Once that state capital was under Confederate control, Lee would move his forces east toward Philadelphia, Baltimore, Maryland, and finally, south to Washington, D.C.

On September 4, the army of Northern Virginia crossed the Potomac River and entered the Union state of Maryland. The spirits of the men were high, but their strength was low. They had fought and marched hard for most of the past year. Now they were hungry and poorly supplied. Barely 40,000 men entered Maryland with Lee, Jackson, and Longstreet. One observer described them as they arrived in the North. "The rebels are wretchedly clad . . . the cavalry men are mostly barefooted, and the feet of the infantry are bound up in rags and pieces of rawhide."

On September 6, the army entered the Maryland town of Frederick. There, General Lee developed a daring plan. Knowing McClellan's slow and cautious style, Lee assumed he had some time before the Union army threatened him. Some 30 miles from Frederick was Harpers Ferry, back under Union control with 14,000 Union soldiers guarding tons of supplies and weapons. Lee wanted to capture the Ferry, but to do so, he had to divide his already small army.

Jackson, Lee decided, would take five divisions and attack Harpers Ferry from three sides, while Longstreet marched part of the army to Hagerstown, keeping another part under D. H. Hill at South Mountain to protect against any possible Union advance. Jackson favored Lee's plan, but Longstreet opposed it, claiming it would allow the Confederates small forces to be destroyed if McClellan came up quickly. Lee was confident McClellan would do nothing quickly.

On September 9, the Confederates withdrew from Frederick to begin their tasks. Soon after, a Union cavalry troop rode into Frederick and discovered one of greatest mysteries of the Civil War. In a field, they found a copy of Lee's battle plan, called Special Order # 191. It was wrapped around three cigars. No one knew where it came from, or from whom. This detailed description of Lee's assignments made its way quickly to George McClellan, who declared, "Here is a paper with which, if I cannot whip Bobbie Lee, I will be willing to go home." McClellan now moved his army toward Hagerstown, Maryland, and the Rebels had no idea of the danger they were in.

Jackson's assignment on September 10 was forbidding. His 14,000 men had to march more than 70 miles, around to the west of Harpers Ferry and back, while defeating Federal troops. Ideally, Lee wanted the job done in five days, including three for taking and evacuating Harpers

★

Lee was known as "Bobbie Lee" as a West Point cadet.

★

Ferry. Jackson's two extra divisions, under Generals Lafayette McLaws and John Walker, would take direct routes and attack the Ferry from the north and south.

By September 13, Jackson had occupied Bolivar Heights, one of the three elevated cliffs above the ferry that made it so difficult to defend. From his earlier days in Harpers Ferry, Jackson knew control of the three highlands meant victory for the South. By the next day, McLaws had taken Maryland Heights, and Walker had captured Loudon Heights. Harpers Ferry was surrounded.

Meanwhile, McClellan had moved quickly to trap Lee. His Army of the Potomac, close to 90,000 men, had caught up to D. H. Hill's rear guard at South Mountain. One section of McClellan's army was sent toward Harpers Ferry to trap McLaws. The rest tried to push through South Mountain to trap Longstreet.

★

Abolitionist John Brown had led a failed attack on Harpers Ferry in 1859.

★

Though Hill was able to hold the Federals off for an entire day, Lee still felt that the invasion had failed. He sent a message to McLaws, informing him that the army would have to pull back across the Potomac. Then, Jackson sent his own message to Lee.

Although the attack on Harpers Ferry had been delayed, Jackson promised it would fall in the morning. Lee decided to hold off retreat.

True to his word, Jackson launched a destructive artillery attack on Harpers Ferry at dawn on September 15. By 9:00 A.M., the Federals had surrendered. As one soldier later wrote, "We were as helpless as rats in a cage." Stonewall Jackson had forced the largest surrender of U.S. troops in the entire Civil War: 12,500 men along with dozens of artillery pieces, hundreds of wagons, and thousands of small arms. When Lee received Jackson's report, he decided to make a stand against McClellan near a town called Sharpsburg, on Antietam Creek. Jackson left A. P. Hill in charge of Harpers Ferry, with instructions to join Lee's army as soon as possible, and by that night, Jackson and the rest of his men were marching the seventeen miles to reach Lee and Longstreet.

At Sharpsburg, Lee pulled his army back together. He would need every man, because his army at Sharpsburg numbered barely 35,000, with another 4,000 at Harpers Ferry under A.P. Hill. McClellan had well over 70,000 men, with thousands more only a few hours' march away. Lee placed Jackson on the Confederate left, with Longstreet in charge of the center and right. The Federal plan called for an attack against Jackson's position at daybreak on September 17, led by Union General "Fighting Joe" Hooker.

The attack began at dawn, and some of the bloodiest fighting of the entire Civil War took place, troops firing point blank into each other's lines, artillery cutting men to pieces. General Hooker later recalled, "It was never my fortune to witness a more bloody, dismal battlefield."

On the Confederate side, Jackson was quickly losing officers. General Starke was killed, as was another brigade leader. General J. R. Jones was badly wounded, along with Colonel James Walker, Jackson's VMI student who had once challenged him to a duel. Jackson sent in the division under General John Bell Hood. They were able to hold off the Union attack but at a high price. Hood lost over 60 percent of his division that morning. As the Union sent in a new corps under General Joseph Mansfield, Lee sent reinforcements to support Jackson.

McClellan added the Union Second Corps, under General Edwin "Bull" Sumner, hoping to crush Jackson. Sumner, however, had a poor understanding of the battle, and he sent a division straight across Jackson's front line. Expecting to meet an enemy in front, the division actually marched until Jackson's men were along their left flank. Realizing the opportunity, the Southern soldiers poured fire into the Federal ranks, who became trapped and ended up shooting one another as often as they shot the Rebels. Within 15 minutes, the Federals lost more than 2,000 men.

Dead soldiers filled the fields after the battle at Antietam, the single bloodiest day of the Civil War.

The overall toll of those first four hours of fighting at Antietam was staggering: almost 13,000 men lay dead or wounded on both sides. Jackson had used every man available to him, and fortunately the destruction of the Federal division marked the end of the worst fighting in his area. At one point, as Jackson was talking to McLaws, a Union shell fell next to them but failed to explode. Jackson said, "God has been very kind to us today." He could have been talking about the shell or about the fact that his men had withstood the Union fury.

The battle shifted farther south, as McClellan's men tested the rest of the Confederate line. After a terrible fight in the Confederate center, at a point called "Bloody Lane," the Union broke the Confederate line but failed to move ahead. Farther south, the Federals finally crossed a bridge over the Antietam Creek and threatened to capture Sharpsburg. This would have cut Jackson off from Lee, Longstreet, and any possible escape across the Potomac.

At the last possible moment, the Union troops were attacked on their left flank by A.P. Hill. His men had supervised the surrender at Harpers Ferry and marched the seventeen miles to Sharpsburg in seven hours just in time to save Lee's army. With the Union pushed back to the creek, the fighting ended for the day.

The next day, both sides stared at each other across the fields, but the fight did not start again.

81

★

On September 22, 1862, President Lincoln issued the Emancipation Proclamation, freeing slaves on January 1, 1863.

★

The battle had been the bloodiest single day of the war—in fact, of any U.S. war, before or since. Almost 23,000 men were injured or killed at Antietam. The Confederacy lost over 10,000—nearly one-third of the men who had fought. Jackson held his position against tremendous pressure, but he did so at high cost—almost 40 percent of his men fell in battle. On the evening of September 18, Lee ordered the army to withdraw across the Potomac.

War in Winter

Back in Virginia, Lee worked to rebuild his battered army. New soldiers poured into the ranks, replacing those injured and killed in Maryland. Lee also decided to create two formal corps, similar to the structure of the Union army. The choice to lead these corps was relatively easy. James Longstreet and Stonewall Jackson were both promoted to Lieutenant General and given command of one corps each. In his letter to President Davis, Lee wrote, "My opinion of the merits of General Jackson has been greatly enhanced during this expedition. He is true, honest and brave; has a single eye to the good of the service and spares no exertion to accomplish his object." No one questioned Stonewall's promotion, though not every soldier was pleased. As one officer wrote home, "I must admit it is much pleasanter to read about Stonewall & his exploits than to serve under him & perform those exploits." Lieutenant General Thomas Jackson now controlled over 32,000 troops in 4 divisions, led by Generals Jubal Early, William Taliaferro, A.P. Hill, and D. H. Hill.

On the Union side, there was little activity. In fact, by November President Lincoln had become so tired of trying to force McClellan to pursue Lee that he replaced him with General Ambrose Burnside. Burnside was given direct instructions to actively continue the war and crush Lee. Even though the winter was approaching, Burnside began to move his massive army south to meet Lee. By the end of November, 78,000 members of the Army of Northern Virginia stood at Fredericksburg, Virginia. Across the Rappahannock River stood 115,000 Federals.

Jackson was prepared to face another fight, but first he had to make some time for personal news. On November 28, he received word that Anna had successfully given birth to a daughter. It was a sign of his tremendous devotion to his duty that he was able to stay at the front. Jackson named the girl Julia Laura, for his mother and his sister. In a letter home, the proud father wrote,

Oh! how thankful I am to our kind Heavenly Father for having spared my precious wife and given us a little daughter! I cannot tell you how gratified I am, nor how much I wish I could be with you and see my two little darlings ... How I would love to see the darling little thing! Give her many kisses for her father.

83

Before meeting his daughter, however, there was a battle to be fought. Though Burnside had made good speed to reach the Rappahannock by mid-November, his drive stalled there. As Burnside waited for material to build pontoon bridges across the river, Lee set his defenses. Finally, on December 11, Burnside began his move. Union soldiers easily occupied the town of Fredericksburg that day, but the Confederates were dug in on the steep hills behind the town. Longstreet's corps controlled the Confederate left directly behind the town on both sides of a hill called Marye's Heights. Jackson's corps, with fewer men but more cannons, was on the right near an area called Hamilton's Crossing.

On December 13, the Union attack began. Burnside aimed his first strikes at Jackson's position on the right. His orders to Union General William Franklin were unclear, and instead of using the 60,000 men in his command, Franklin only used about 4,500 men in his attack. Three divisions, under Generals George Meade, John Gibbon, and Abner Doubleday, began the attack. They were quickly hit by Confederate artillery, and Doubleday's division stopped its advance.

General Abner Doubleday

Union artillery pounded Jackson's position for the next hour, and on Jackson's order, the Confederate guns fell silent. Convinced that they had destroyed the Rebels' cannons, the Union troops renewed their attack: straight into the teeth of fifty cannons. At only 800 yards, the Union troops were cut to shreds by exploding canister shot. They looked for the nearest cover, which happened to be the edge of a wooded area to their right. A.P. Hill had chosen to leave that area undefended, because he thought the land was too marshy. When the Union troops reached it, they were between two Confederate brigades. Though the Yankees did some severe damage to one brigade, Jackson was able to bring up strong reinforcements and push them back.

After failing against Jackson, Burnside concentrated on Longstreet on the Confederate left. Here, Lee's position was even stronger; his men were on high ground in a protected spot, and Confederate artillery could dominate the entire area. As one cannoneer bragged, "A chicken could not live on that field when we open (fire) on it." Though the Union launched at least fourteen brigades against the Confederate troops on Marye's Heights, not one Yankee soldier reached the top. By the end of the day, Burnside's battered army had moved back from the attack after suffering 12,600 casualties to only 5,300 for the Confederates. The two armies remained in place for two days, and many Union wounded froze to death in the land between the forces. By December 16, Burnside had withdrawn back across the Rappahannock.

★

Seeing his Rebels celebrate at Fredericksburg, Lee said, "It is well that war is so terrible or we would grow too fond of it."

★

85

Chapter 6

THE FINAL BATTLE

The next three months passed quietly. General Burnside made one attempt to re-cross the river, but heavy rains forced him back. Soon after, President Lincoln replaced Burnside with General Joseph "Fighting Joe" Hooker. Although he was called "immoral" and a "drunkard" by many, Hooker expected to turn the Army of the Potomac back into a strong fighting machine. After his appointment in late January, he began to reorganize his force and prepare for a great strike.

OPPOSITE: Jackson leads his men at Chancellorsville.

Jackson, meanwhile, took the quiet time to tend to other matters. He wrote most of his official battle reports during this time. He also brought his wife and daughter up to his camp. It was the first time he had ever seen his daughter. His wife, Anna, described the meeting:

> His face was all sunshine and gladness; and, after greeting his wife, it was a picture, indeed, to see his look of perfect delight and admiration as his eyes fell upon that baby... His face reflected all the happiness and delight that were in his heart.

On April 23, he had the baby baptized, but less than a week later, word arrived that Hooker's army had begun to move. With regret, Jackson sent Anna and Julia to Richmond. He had seen them for nine days.

Hooker knew that Lee had sent Longstreet with part of his army south to gather supplies and help guard Richmond and the coast. This left Lee with fewer than 60,000 men available, while Hooker had over 134,000. Still, Hooker was smart enough not to repeat Burnside's error and attack the Confederates' strong positions near Fredericksburg. Instead, Hooker sent most of his forces upstream to circle around the Rebels and attack them from the side and rear.

When Lee heard of the Union movement, he sent General Richard Anderson's division out to

★

On April 16, 1863, Admiral David Porter lead a flotilla of Union gunboats past the Rebel defenses at Vicksburg on the Mississippi River.

★

Stonewall Jackson

Anna and Julia Jackson

★ ★ ★ ★ ★

Jackson's second wife, Anna Morrison, was the daughter of Robert Morrison, the founder of Davidson College in North Carolina. She was sister-in-law to Daniel Harvey Hill, who fought with Jackson in Mexico and in the early years of the Civil War. Hill first introduced Anna Morrison and Thomas Jackson. Jackson and Anna sent a regular stream of letters to each other when they were separated—letters full of affection and devotion. After Jackson's death, Anna returned to North Carolina. Called the "Widow of the Confederacy," Anna was well loved and respected throughout her life. She died in 1915 at the age of eighty-three, and was buried in Lexington next to Thomas.

Julia Laura Jackson only met her father twice briefly as an infant. In the 1870s, she changed her name to Julia Thomas Jackson, to honor her father and because Jackson's sister, Laura, had been a Unionist during the war. She married William Christian in 1885, and they had two children. Julia died of typhoid fever in 1889 at the age of twenty-six. Her children, however, had several children of their own, and Thomas Jackson has numerous descendents today.

Julia Jackson

investigate. At a road junction called Chancellorsville, near the edge of a tangled mass of trees and shrubs called the Wilderness, Anderson found Hooker's army. Hopelessly outnumbered, Anderson had his men dig in as he sent a message back to Lee asking for aid. Lee and Jackson briefly considered withdrawing in the face of such odds, but decided instead to attack the Yankees. On May 1, Jackson led his men to the Wilderness to support Anderson. There, outnumbered five to one, Jackson attacked.

Hooker was shocked. He had completed what some called the most successful march of the war, sneaking around Lee. Never humble, he had sent a message to Lincoln: "My plans are perfect, and when I start to carry them out, may God have mercy on General Lee, for I will have none." Now, not only were the Confederates not retreating, they were attacking him. Confused and perhaps unnerved by the attack, Hooker pulled his troops back to Chancellorsville and took up a defensive position.

The Last March

That night, Lee and Jackson discussed their options. Lee proposed one of the most daring moves of the war, and Jackson quickly agreed. Taking two thirds of Lee's army, Jackson would copy Hooker's feat, but in less time and more secrecy. He would march around Hooker while Lee kept the Union's attention to their front. Then,

Jackson could attack from the rear, and trap the Union between his men and Lee's. Already badly outnumbered, the Confederates could be completely destroyed if Hooker attacked while they were divided. Still, both Confederate generals felt this was the only hope for a victory.

★

The road on which Jackson's troops march was so narrow that the Rebel force stretched out nearly 10 miles.

★

At 7:30 on the morning of May 2, Jackson ordered his 28,000 men to begin a twelve-mile hike through the heavy vegetation and thick forest of the Wilderness. Union scouts discovered the march, but Hooker assumed it was the Confederate retreat he had predicted. Jackson pushed his men as hard as he ever had, even giving up his usual ten-minute break in every hour.

By 5:00 P.M. the Confederates were ready. The dense Wilderness hid them from view, and the

Generals Lee and Jackson planned strategy at Chancellorsville.

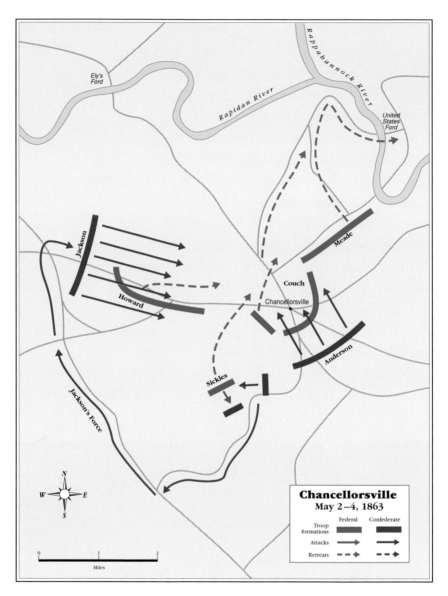

Chancellorsville
May 2–4, 1863

	Federal	Confederate
Troop formations	▬	▬
Attacks	→	→
Retreats	--→	--→

nearby Union troops had no idea of their immediate danger. First came a series of bugle calls, softened by the deep woods. Then came the "Rebel Yell," the intense, fierce screams of the Confederates as they launched their attack.

A Southern artillery officer watched the fight begin.

The surprise was complete. A bolt from the sky would not have startled (the Federals) as much as the muskets shots . . . There was nothing left to do but to lay down their arms and surrender, or flee. They threw them away, and fled . . . Men lost their heads in terror.

Stonewall Jackson was a master at inspiring his men during battle.

The Confederates were so successful that some units pushed well ahead of others. Sometime after 7:00 P.M., Jackson had to call a halt to the attack. He knew the Union was badly confused and could be hurt further, but darkness, confusion, the Wilderness, and exhaustion kept him from pushing his men onward. Still, he wanted to know where the Federals were, to prepare for his next attack.

Taking a group of staff officers, he began to form a plan for another attack that night. Soon joined by A.P. Hill and staff, Jackson, Hill and seventeen staff officers rode off in front of the Confederate forces to scout the land and the Union positions.

However, because of Jackson's firm belief in keeping information private, word of the scouting party's direction was not passed to all units. Eventually, the group began to ride back toward Confederate lines.

93

The confusion and darkness made the Rebel units nervous. The 18th North Carolina, listening to the nearby shots, suddenly heard a group of riders approaching their front line through the dark woods. One shot rang out, then several more, then a large volley. Of the nineteen men including Jackson and Hill, ten were hit by bullets from their own troops. Stonewall Jackson was shot three times: twice in his left arm and once in his right hand. As A.P. Hill, miraculously unhurt, managed to get the North Carolina troops to stop their fire, men hurried to help Jackson.

Dr. Samuel B. Morrison, the brother of Mary Anna Jackson, examined Jackson after he was wounded in 1863.

Still conscious, Jackson knew his arm was badly shattered by the bullets. Hill sat with Jackson as a message was sent to find Dr. McGuire. Soon, Union artillery began to fire. Hill, now in command of Jackson's corps, rode off to take charge of the battle. Moments later, Hill was wounded by an artillery shell. Men began to move Jackson away from the fighting, but at least twice he was dropped as bullets and shells fell too close.

Finally, Jackson was carried through the woods to a tavern, where Surgeon McGuire caught up with him. In response to McGuire's concern, Jackson answered "I am badly injured, Doctor. I fear I am dying." McGuire's examination showed a severed artery

94

which had caused a huge loss of blood. Though the doctor stopped the immediate bleeding, Jackson was in critical condition. Still concerned about the Union guns, McGuire had Jackson moved again, to a tavern farther away from the fight. At 2:00 A.M. McGuire amputated Jackson's left arm, hoping to save his life.

With the loss of both Jackson and Hill, control of the corps had passed to Jeb Stuart who continued the fight on May 3. After hours of brutal struggle, second only to Antietam in the total number of casualties in a day, the Union was pushed back across the Rappahannock. Many Confederates shouted "Revenge Jackson" as they fought. The North lost more than 18,000 men compared to the Confederates' loss of 12,800. Though some called the Battle of Chancellorsville Lee's greatest victory, the price was too high. Short of losing Lee himself, the loss of Stonewall Jackson was the worst possible blow for the Confederate army.

Jackson awoke that day feeling much better. He sent an aide to Richmond to bring Anna to his side, and generally tried to keep track of the battle. On May 4, Lee had Jackson moved again, farther from any possible battle. Friends of Jackson's, the Chandlers, had a home near Guiney's Station. There, Jackson was placed in a cottage where he could have quiet. For the next two days, he seemed to improve.

After midnight on May 7, Jackson awoke with what Dr. McGuire most feared—signs of

Life and Death in Jackson's Time

★ ★ ★ ★ ★

Although he suffered a great deal of personal tragedy and died an early death, Stonewall Jackson's experiences were not unusual. In the nineteenth century, disease and death were constant companions in everyday life. The death of Jackson's father and sister from typhoid fever, for example, was not an uncommon occurrence.

Today we know that typhoid fever is caused by a bacteria found in human wastes that is spread through unclean food and drinking water or by contact with an infected person. Modern sewage systems and vaccinations have almost eradicated the deadly disease in the United States. But in Jackson's time, before people knew that germs cause disease, a high fever followed by rosy spots on the chest usually meant death.

More than 75,000 cases of typhoid fever alone were reported during the Civil War. In fact, many historians attribute the Union defeat during the peninsula campaign—Lee's first victory—to the fact that Northern troops were so weakened by typhoid fever that they could not fight. Even President Lincoln was affected by typhoid—his beloved son, Willie, died in 1862 at age eleven from the disease.

Jackson's first wife died during childbirth, which was also not an unusual event in the 1800's. An illness known as puerpal fever often appeared mysteriously after deliveries and often led to quick deaths of both mother and child. Doctors were unable to prevent puerperal fever until the 1880s, when they understood that unclean instruments and doctors' unwashed hands had a direct correlation to the high rate of death in childbirth.

The amputation of Jackson's arm after he was shot was not unusual either. The development of conical bullets, known as minié balls, led to enormous numbers of amputations during the Civil War. Minié balls were made of soft lead that distorted on impact, shattering bone and causing huge wounds that pressed soiled fabric and other dirt into the area. Setting splintered bone and closing the wound was impossible in many cases. Amputation was the quickest and safest medical practice for wounds to the extremities.

Amputations, such as this one being performed in front of a hospital tent at Gettysburg, were common during the Civil War.

pneumonia. Because there were no antibiotics at the time, this infection of the lungs was often fatal. McGuire did everything he could to heal Jackson. Word went to General Lee, who had originally been told that Jackson's wounds were not as serious as some thought. Lee now sent a message with a courier: "Give General Jackson my affectionate regards and say to him: he has lost his left arm but I my right arm. Tell him to get well and come back to me as soon as he can."

At noon that day, Anna and Julia arrived. The next day, May 8, Jackson alternated between good spirits and delirium. At times, he shouted battle orders, but he also had serious and affectionate conversations with Anna and McGuire. By May 9, those closest to Jackson had given up hope for his recovery. At one point, he looked up and said, "You think my condition dangerous, but I thank God, if it is His will, that I am ready to go. I am not afraid to die."

On May 10, Julia Jackson was brought to her father for one final visit. Later Jackson, discovering that the day was Sunday, said, "It is the Lord's day. My wish is fulfilled. I have always desired to die on Sunday."

By noon, Jackson was in a coma, broken only by occasional orders as he rejoined his troops in his mind. "Order A.P. Hill to prepare for action! Pass the Infantry to the front!" he called out. Then for a while he was quiet again. At 3:15, he quietly said, "Let us pass over the river, and rest under the shade of the trees." Those were his final words; Thomas "Stonewall" Jackson was dead.

To the Confederate army and the Confederacy as a whole, the news was devastating. As word spread through camp "the sounds of merriment died away as if the Angel of Death himself had flapped his muffled wings over the troops . . . many were the veterans . . . whose bronzed cheeks were now wet with burning tears."

Most people were simply heartbroken, however, some realized the impact Jackson's death could have on the entire war. One citizen said this "was the first time it had dawned on us that God would let us be defeated." On the Union side, feelings were understandably different: "We shall fear him no more" said a soldier from Massachusetts.

Jackson's body was brought to Richmond, where all flags flew at half mast and church bells pealed. A newly designed Confederate flag, the first ever made, was draped over Jackson's coffin. Jackson lay in state in Richmond for two days, then was taken to Lexington. On May 15, Stonewall Jackson was buried at VMI, in his beloved Shenandoah Valley.

Thomas Jackson died at age 39, at the height of his fame and at the worst possible moment for the Confederacy. Lee used the momentum of the Chancellorsville victory to launch his second invasion of the North, an invasion that would end in Confederate defeat at Gettysburg, Pennsylvania. Some historians have argued that Stonewall Jackson

VMI cadets surround Jackson's grave, at VMI in the Shenandoah Valley.

might have been able to win at Gettysburg, or at least could have convinced Lee not to fight there.

Though he was a hero to many in the Confederacy, the men who served under Stonewall Jackson knew he was not a perfect commander. He was a demanding leader, a poor communicator, and often insensitive to his men's feelings and needs. He was, however, a great general in a terrible war, one whose men followed him without question.

★

On May 18, 1863, Union forces surrounded Vicksburg, Mississippi. The siege would last until July 4.

★

With Stonewall Jackson leading them, the Confederates felt like they could do anything. Without him, their cause seemed doomed.

This man of deep faith gave his men faith that they could overcome any odds and achieve any task if they set themselves to it. In his own odd, shy, quiet way, this brave man became one of the most unforgettable figures in the Civil War.

Stonewall Jackson

Glossary

abolitionism a political movement in the 1800s that sought to ban slavery

amputation surgical removal of a shattered extremity

artillery large weapons used by fighting forces that fall into three categories—guns or cannons, howitzers, and mortars

brevet Promotion of a military officer in rank with a rise in pay or responsibility

brigade a military unit smaller than a division, usually consisting of three to five regiments of 500 to 1,000 soldiers

casualties the total number of soldiers dead, wounded, and missing after a battle

commander a military leader, usually holding the rank of general

corps a military grouping of between 10,000 and 20,000 soldiers

compromise a settlement reached by mutual agreement of two opposing sides on an issue

division a military grouping of between 6,000 and 8,000 soldiers or two to three brigades

emancipation freedom

ford a crossing on a stream or river

malaria a disease caused by mosquito bites

plantation a large farm in the South worked by slaves in the years before the Civil War

quartermaster officer in charge of providing food, clothing, shelter, and other basic supplies

regiment a military unit smaller than a brigade and a division. In the Civil War soldiers fought in the same regiment throughout the war with fellow soldiers who were usually from the same state, city, or town

101

reinforce in military terms, to strengthen a military unit by
  sending in fresh troops

secede to break away

typhoid an often-fatal disease caused by contaminated
  drinking water

Unionist one who believes that the states should remain
  united

For More Information

Web Sites

Stonewall Jackson's Home Page
http://norfacad.pvt.k12.va.us/project/sjackson/sjackson.htm
A detailed biography as well as links to other topics of
interest regarding the Civil War.

Stonewall Jackson Resources at the Virginia Military Institute
http://www.vmi.edu/~archtml/jackson.html
An excellent collection of images, writings, and biographical
detail.

Stonewall Jackson Shrine
http://www.nps.gov/frsp/js.htm
A national Park Service web site link from the
Fredericksburg page provides a great deal of information
about Jackson's final days as well as links to key people and
events in Jackson's brief but fabled career.

The Stonewall Brigade
http://www.stonewallbrigade.com/
A web site about the soldiers who fought under Jackson with
images and other information as well as articles about
modern reenactments of Civil War battles fought by the
brigade.

102

Books

Henderson, G.F.R. *Stonewall Jackson*. New York: Smithmark Press, 1994.

Jackson, Mary Anna. *Life and Letters of Stonewall Jackson*. Harrisonburg: Sprinkle Publications.

Jackson, Mary Anna. *Memoirs of Thomas J. Jackson*. Dayton: Morningside Press, 1993.

Krick, Robert. *Conquering the Valley*. New York: William Morrow & Co., 1996.

Robertson, James I. *Stonewall Jackson: The Man, the Soldier, the Legend*. Atlanta: MacMillan Publications, 1997.

Sears, Stephen. *Chancellorsville*. New York: Houghton Mifflin, 1996.

Tanner, Robert G. *Stonewall in the Valley*. Mechanicsburg: Stackpole Books, 1996.

Vandiver, Frank E. *Mighty Stonewall*. College Station: Texas A&M University Press, 1995.

Index